ICME-13 Topical Surveys

Series editor

Gabriele Kaiser, Faculty of Education, University of Hamburg, Hamburg, Germany

More information about this series at http://www.springer.com/series/14352

Stephen Hegedus · Colette Laborde
Corey Brady · Sara Dalton
Hans-Stefan Siller · Michal Tabach
Jana Trgalova · Luis Moreno-Armella

Uses of Technology in Upper Secondary Mathematics Education

Stephen Hegedus
Dean of School of Education
Southern Connecticut State University
Connecticut, CT
USA

Colette Laborde
Cabrilog
Fontaine
France

Corey Brady
Vanderbilt University
Nashville, TN
USA

Sara Dalton
Mathematics Department
University of Massachusetts
  Dartmouth
Massachusetts, MA
USA

Hans-Stefan Siller
Mathematisches Institut
University of Koblenz and Landau
Koblenz
Germany

Michal Tabach
School of Education
Tel Aviv University
Tel Aviv, Tel Aviv
Israel

Jana Trgalova
Maître de Conférences
Claude Bernard University
Lyon
France

Luis Moreno-Armella
Cinvestav-IPN
Mexico D.F.
Mexico

ISSN 2366-5947   ISSN 2366-5955   (electronic)
ICME-13 Topical Surveys
ISBN 978-3-319-42610-5   ISBN 978-3-319-42611-2   (eBook)
DOI 10.1007/978-3-319-42611-2

Library of Congress Control Number: 2016945848

Printed on acid-free paper

This Springer imprint is published by Springer Nature
The registered company is Springer International Publishing AG Switzerland

Main Topics You Can Find in This "ICME-13 Topical Survey"

- Digital dynamic representations and cognition;
- Sharing mathematical knowledge and collaborative learning with technology
- Emerging technologies;
- Mathematical activities enhanced by technology at upper secondary school;
- New teacher competencies required by the use of technology and teacher education.

Contents

Uses of Technology in Upper Secondary Mathematics Education

1 Introduction

The use of technology in upper secondary mathematics education is a multifaceted topic. This topical survey addresses several dimensions of the topic and attempts at referring to international research studies as it is written by a team of several authors from five countries of three different continents. The survey is structured into four subchapters, each of them addressing a theme of the TSG 43 at ICME 13.

- Technology in secondary mathematics education: theory
  Technology is often arousing enthusiasm as well as reluctance among teachers and mathematics educators. Therefore it was necessary to start the survey with a theoretical analysis of features of digital technologies from an epistemological and a cognitive perspective. A unique epistemological feature of mathematics is their symbolic dimension. It is impossible to gain direct access to mathematical objects as to physical objects. The only way is to access them is through representations. Digital technologies mediate mathematics and some of them offer new kinds of representations, like dynamic and socially distributed representations. Based on a Vygostkian perspective and an instrumentation approach, the use of digital technologies is analyzed as a coaction or a creative interplay between tool and human and as social coaction with socially distributed technology. This theoretical analysis is presented in the first subchapter and the second subchapter also refers to it.

- The role of new technologies: changing interactions
  Part of the role of new technologies is to change the process toward an outcome for learning. This process includes developing a mathematical discourse, providing opportunities to conjecture and test, and active not passive learning. New technologies can add to these processes by connecting learners in different ways with each other and the phenomena under study, mediating learning in different ways, and can offer the opportunity for students to build on the work of one

S. Hegedus et al., *Uses of Technology in Upper Secondary Mathematics Education*, ICME-13 Topical Surveys, DOI 10.1007/978-3-319-42611-2_1

another through the ability to share products or problem solving strategies. In particular technologies offering mobility, multimodality (using various sensory modalities: sight, touch, sound) and connectivity can support student learning. The knowledge and practices that result from the process of learning using digital technologies might be new. Through operationalizing the definition of "new" in terms of how we interact with the learning environment, three organizing principles structures this subchapter: 1. Advances in Activity Spaces, 2. Multimodality, and 3. Moving from *Outside to Inside* the classroom.

- Interrelations between technology and mathematics
  Digital tools support visualization of mathematical concepts in various ways of expressions, and as such may foster versatile thinking, especially when these representations are dynamically linked. At the upper secondary education, these tools can be used for exploring and discovering mathematical correlations and for modeling real complex phenomena. New possibilities are offered by the combination of different environments like CAS and dynamic mathematics environments.
  The use of all these possibilities foster processes that cannot be developed so well in absence of technology, for example: exploration and experimentation, interpretation processes or checking processes. A major consequence is that teaching should be organized differently. Those issues are discussed in the third subchapter.

- Teacher education with technology: what, how and why?
  The preceding subchapters show that teachers need new knowledge and skills to efficiently use technology in upper secondary education. The institutional demands differ from the required teacher competencies elicited by research studies. Usually the institutional demands are not subject matter specific whereas often research studies link a specific type of technology with a mathematical domain. There are many attempts for organizing professional development developing new knowledge and skills, especially in interaction with research. The evaluation of these courses may vary deeply from dissatisfaction to successful outcomes. The theoretical frameworks and research methods on professional development of teachers in using technology as well as their rationale are also presented in this subchapter.

2 Survey

2.1 Technology in Secondary Mathematics Education: Theory

2.1.1 The Challenges of Mathematical Reference

As we approach mathematical cognition in classroom learning environments, the symbolic dimension of mathematics becomes sharply salient. Mathematical discourse is always social, always culturally situated and always shaped by its institutional context; thus the semiotic dimension is always important. However, in learning settings the nature of mathematical objects is very often in question and not (yet) taken-as-shared, so that efforts to evoke these objects and to communicate clearly about them receive particular attention and social pressure.

As a way of framing the problems involved in the relationships between mathematical representations and objects, consider Magritte's *The Treachery of Images*. This famous painting explores issues of representation, in ways that are relevant to mathematical representations. The artist has written "Ceci n'est pas une pipe" ("This is not a pipe"), in painted script, under the painted image of a pipe. The focus is on the viewer's idea of a pipe: within the painting, there are two explicit "pipes"—the pictorial image *of* a pipe and the painted words "une pipe." The painting puts these two "pipes" in conversation with one another and with the viewer's *Pipe* idea. The image falls short of the idea: it is "not a pipe"—one cannot hold it, fill it with tobacco, or smoke it.

Now suppose, instead of a pipe, Magritte had painted a *circle* with the inscribed legend, "Ceci n'est pas un cercle." A different dynamic would have emerged. Magritte would not, even in theory, have been able to reach into his pocket and produce the geometric *circle* that had served as the model for the painting, and that the painted image is *not*. In fact, one might argue that the legend, "Ceci n'est pas un cercle" would be *false*: at least in the sense that every representation of a circle *does* express circle-ness in some degree, and that, further, nothing *except* a collection of such representations does so.

This essentially symbolic dimension of mathematical thought and discourse highlights a unique epistemological feature. Because mathematical objects cannot be *pointed at* independently of its manifestations within one or more representations, mathematical work and mathematical learning must occur in settings that are entirely mediated by representations. This raises the importance of *symbolic production* in the learning process, both as learners formulate their thoughts and as teachers and they exchange symbols and representations in attempting to create shared meanings and understandings. Duval (1999) remarks that "the use of systems of semiotic representation for mathematical thinking is essential because, unlike the other fields of [scientific] knowledge (botany, geology, astronomy, physics), there is no other way of gaining access to mathematical objects but to produce some semiotic representations" (p.4).[1]

2.1.2 The Permanence of Symbolic Beings

Although mathematical objects are wholly symbolic beings that can only be found, expressed, or conjured up through representations, this also paradoxically gives

---

[1]We amend Duval's text by adding "scientific" because the forms of knowledge in the arts and the humanities, for example, do also face the challenge that the objects of their study are inextricably embedded in semiotic/symbolic representations.

them a permanence that cannot be achieved by physical beings or objects. Indeed, they connect with and express very general features of the human experience of the world. This is why, if we were to read in the newspaper tomorrow morning that the Natural Numbers had been destroyed in a fire, we would smile. We know this is not possible, even though there are many instances of representations of the Natural Numbers in perishable material media.

Part of the reason for the more enduring nature of symbolic entities like the Natural Numbers is the very fact that they do not refer directly to specific objects in the physical or cultural world. That is, the representational and symbolic challenges with which we opened this discussion are also sources of mathematical power. To understand the nature and power of symbolic entities, we can look first at how they emerged in human history and then at how they operate in modern discourse.

2.1.3 The Emergence of Symbolic Entities

Among the first symbolic entities in human history may have been the records that have been found scratched in bones and dating from about 35 thousand years ago. These marks may have been used to keep track of the number of animals killed in a hunt or the number of days in a lunar cycle. Any external mark or trace that carried and communicated meaning was already a symbolic object: that is, a thing whose purpose was to represent another thing. Moreover, it was perhaps the infeasibility of making an iconographic symbol that led these early humans to produce representations that were loosely coupled to the particular animals or days they described, capturing instead the notion of quantity. The loose coupling of the symbol to its referent made it possible to see relations between two such symbols, even when there was no relation between the objects whose quantities these symbols represented. Thus, the "five-ness" of five sheep, five days, or five pieces of fruit could come to be represented, rather than, and independently of the "sheepness", the "dayness" or the "fruitiness" of the objects. In this way, the number five came to be lifted off of the concrete groups of objects that it described, to gain the status of an independent symbolic entity. A symbol can be thought of as a crystallized action—in this case the action of counting.

As symbolic entities, mathematical objects have a doubly paradoxical relation to the physical world. They exist on a different plane from physical objects, having been decoupled from that world through processes of abstraction and generalization. Moreover, as we have suggested, they cannot be depicted directly or completely. Instead, through representations, certain facets of symbolic entities can be captured, but it is in the nature of generalized symbolic entities that they supersede any particular representation. For instance, consider the mathematical symbolic entity of a straight line. In a geometric drawing, we can represent the line as an object in a plane. Applying a coordinate system, we can produce the equation of that line, another representation. Neither of these two representations of the line encompasses the entire mathematical nature of the line; yet each of which captures a facet of its nature. In general, each system of representation reveals an aspect of the mathematical entities it describes, and each conceals or leaves behind other aspects. Thus the choice of a representation is always a consequential choice that constitutes the view and access we have to mathematical object.

Symbolic entities shared some features with early concrete physical tools, while they also differed from early tools in other respects. Vygotsky's (1978) famous analysis of this relation was that while tools enabled humans to operate on and exert control over the world, symbolic entities also enabled humans to exert control over themselves and regulate their own internal thinking processes-being a central part of these processes. In coming to operate with tools and symbolic entities, human beings gained enormous new powers. Donald (2001) describes this process as the advent of "theoretical culture" and it is the centerpiece of the Baldwinian inter-pretation of cultural evolution (Baldwin 1896). With tools, humans encoded pro-cesses of labor and craft in physical objects, which afforded (Gibson 2014) the actions that constituted those processes. In this way, tools began to structure human society, so that emerging habits of mind, ways of life, and classes of society were reflected and transmitted in the characteristics sets of tools that supported them. Thus, these extensions to human nature also supported intergenerational develop-ment, capturing successful innovations in a transmission medium more flexible and more easily shareable than the biological substrate of DNA. With the symbolic system of written language, communications could be detached from particular interpersonal contacts, enabling new forms of literature, history, science, and phi-losophy. And with the symbolic system of mathematical discourse, the study of abstract form and structure could take shape and transcend the lives of individual thinkers.

2.1.4 Mediated Activity

This shift in human history is so significant that now many thinkers view human activity as essentially and distinctively mediated activity (e.g., Wertsch 1991):

> The most central claim I wish to pursue is that human action typically employs mediational means such as tools and language and that these mediational means shape the action in essential ways (p. 12).

For instance, consider the relationship between an expert musician and her instrument, as, for example in Jacqueline du Pré's rendering of Elgar's cello con-certo. During the performance, the artist and the instrument appear to become one. It is certainly not the case that the performance appears effortless; the striking thing about it is that it appears to be co-produced by the musician and the instrument. It seems incorrect to describe the performance as "Du Pré playing on the cello;" instead, it seems appropriate to say, "Du Pré and her cello co-produced the music." Moreover, "her cello" here represents the conceptual image of the cello that Du Pré was able to internalize over the course of many years of hard, reflective practice. There is fluidity in this human-artifact integration, making the cello acquire a sound and texture distinctive to the artist (that is, the source of the music is Du Pré and her cello"). We use the term co-action (Moreno-Armella and Hegedus 2009) to describe this generative and creative interplay between humans and tools or symbol systems.

Gleick's (1993) biography of Richard Feynman records an exchange between Feynman and the historian Charles Weiner. Feynman reacted sharply to Weiner's statement that Feynman's notes offer "a record" of his "day-to-day work."

> "I actually did the work on paper", Feynman said.

> "Well," Weiner said, "the work was done in your head, but the record of it is still here."

> "No, it's not a record, not really. It's working. You have to work on paper, and this is the paper. Okay?" (Gleick 1993, p. 409)

The distinction that Feynman makes here shows how he sees his work as intrinsically interconnected with the symbolic system that he is working with. His ideas do not occur separately from their realization in written symbols; rather, they emerge through interaction with that symbol system. It is the same as with Du Pré and her cello, where there is no music without both the artist and the instrument being present.

Indeed, the process of coming to be able to operate fluently and effectively with tools and symbols is common to all learners as they appropriate the practices and "habits of mind" of a discipline. The human mind (and indeed the human brain) re-forms itself to accommodate these new discipline-specific ways of operating. For instance, Donald (2001, p. 302) has explained that literacy skills transform the functional architecture of the brain and have a profound impact on how literate people perform their cognitive work. The complex neural components of a literate vocabulary, Donald explains, have to be built into the brain through years of schooling to rewire the functional organization of our thinking. Similar processes take place when we appropriate numbers at school. It is easy to multiply 7 by 8 without representational supports, but if we want to multiply 12,345 by 78,654 then we write the numbers down and follow the specific rules of the multiplication algorithm. It is because we have been able to internalize reading and writing and the decimal system, that we are able to perform the corresponding operations with an understanding of their meaning.

2.1.5 Democratizing Access to Co-action

Nevertheless, the kind of rich and generative interplay between mind, tool, and symbolic system that we see with Du Pré and Feynman have historically been accessible only to the maestros of a discipline. A key question for the design of technology-enhanced learning environments is whether the cognitive tools that have been developed in the last 30 years might play a role in democratizing access to this generative mode of interacting with disciplinary structures.

If the most sophisticated users of representations and symbolic systems in the past have been able to engage in active and creative interplay with these systems, it is in part because they were able to create a dynamic relationship between their thinking and inquiry on one hand and the symbolic system on the other. This is possible because they have internalized the system so thoroughly that they are able to mentally simulate it as a dynamic field of potential, enabling them to engage in "what-if" interactions of an exploratory, conversational form. In mathematics, this ability is particularly powerful, because of the dependence on representations that we have described above.

We will describe several classes of technology environments that provide dynamic and/or socially-distributed interfaces with important representational systems in mathematics. These environments offer the potential for learners (even very young learners) to enter into a relationship with those systems, which we describe as co-action. We argue that the experience of relationships of co-action with mathematical structures can contribute to a transformative educational program. Of course, we do not argue that a technology that opens a possibility for co-action is sufficient in itself to give learners access to mathematical understandings that were the hard-won rewards of a lifetime of study for mathematicians of the past. However, we do suggest that carefully planned educational experiences with such environments can remove barriers to broader participation in a culture of mathematical literacy and fluency.

Extreme care is necessary here, as the long history of teaching and learning with static representations should not be ignored in the work to envision its future successor. Instead, we must proceed by pondering how digital and socially distributed representations of mathematical entities can contribute in new ways to genuine mathematical understanding. We see digital and shared representations as capable of adding dimensions to static representational systems and further improving the cycle of: exploration, conjecture, explanation, and justification. Moreover, as educational systems incorporate such environments and experiences, traditional pathways of learning—will gradually give way to new cultural and institutional structures that realize the potential of these innovations. In the sections below, we give two brief examples of co-action, one emphasizing dynamic representations, and the other highlighting socially distributed representations.

2.1.6 Co-action with Dynamic Digital Representations

Consider the family of triangles ABC (Fig. 1a) whose side AC contains a given point P in the interior of angle B. The particular triangle in which A and C are chosen so that P is the midpoint of side AC has the least area among all possible triangles.

We explored this situation with teachers, making use of a dynamic geometry environment (in this case GeoGebra). Beginning from triangle ABC (Fig. 1a), the teachers built a construction that allowed them to vary a point H along the side BA, thus determining a point D on BC for which triangle HBD included point P. Experimenting with the diagram and watching the area measure, they began to believe that the proposition about minimum area was true. Nevertheless, significant doubt remained. Following the logic of the construction, the teachers then extended

Fig. 1 a Finding the triangle with the least area, **b** Introducing a graphical representation of the value of the area changing with placements of vertices along the rays BA and BC

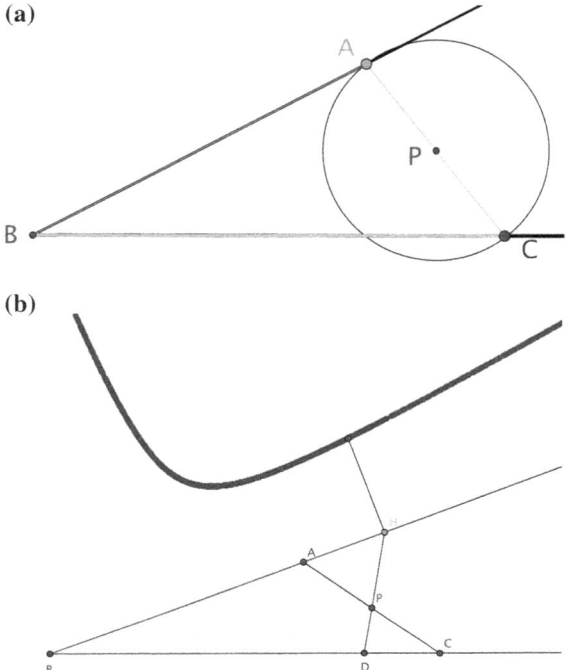

the aspect of their sketch that hinged on the dependency relation between point H and area. They used the length BH as the domain of a function that at each point delivers the area of the corresponding triangle (Fig. 1b). Of course we could have—and we did—graph the function using a traditional coordinate system as well. But we show the hybrid Euclidean/Cartesian construction that emerged because we want to emphasize the possibilities that digital media offer learners to manipulate the objects under study, in service of exploring and building conjectures.

The interaction between learners and dynamic geometry environments can be theoretically addressed in terms of the complex process Rabardel (1995) studied under the name instrumental genesis, which casts light on the mutually defining relationships between a learner and the artifact she is trying to incorporate into her strategies for solving problems. Initially the learner feels the resistance the artifact opposes but eventually she can drive it. In the case of GeoGebra, teachers needed to understand, in particular, the syntactical rules inherent to the software in order to use the medium as a mediator of mathematical knowledge. For this to happen, there must be a melody to be played, that is, teachers need an appropriate mathematical task. This task acts as an incentive to integrate in meaningful ways the dynamic power of the symbolic artifact with their own intellectual resources. If this happens, we say with Rabardel, that the artifact has become an instrument and the activity for solving problems in partnership with it, becomes an instrumented activity.

In such activities the mobility of the dynamic digital representation becomes a crucial feature of the represented entity for the learner. Exploring what remains invariant under dragging, for instance, reveals structural aspects of mathematical objects: motion and invariance enable us to see structure. Importantly, too, the motion is induced by the learner, who takes advantage of the executability of the digital representation to reveal structure and meaning. Perceiving structure through motion is a deeply embodied act—similar to how the bird sees the moth as the latter moves on the bark of the tree. These features, absent from static symbolic representations, help the learner to develop new strategies as she explores mathematical problems. Moreover, they are particularly important for the mathematics taught at upper school, supporting a focus on variables and functions. The digital representation here becomes a semiotic mediator—that is, an artifact that supports the creation of meaning in the mathematical system and its objects. Because the interaction depends on the particular learner's ways of thinking, there is also a strong social dimension to this co-action. The learner makes sense in the context of others, and also through others—co-acting together.

2.1.7 Co-action with Socially-Distributed Representations

Even apparently individual co-action becomes social as learners work together to process the meaning of representations. However, the social dimension can become even more pronounced through collective work with distributed representations. Our second example of co-action involves students interacting collaboratively with the representation and communication infrastructure (Hegedus and Moreno-Armella 2009) of a classroom network of graphing calculators. Within that setting, we can give each student control of a single point in a Cartesian environment, which she can move using the calculator's arrow keys. In real time, the points of all the students in the class are displayed in a shared Cartesian space, which is projected at the front of the classroom. The following activity was created by a teacher to support the idea of the perpendicular bisector of a segment as the locus of points equidistant from the segment's endpoints. As students move their point (point C), they see it represented on their calculator screen as the third vertex of a triangle with the segment AB as its opposite side, where the measures of the variable sides of the triangle are also shown (Fig. 2a, c). The teacher asks the class to search for points where the distances from point C to points A and B are the same.[2] As students locate points that satisfy the condition, a pattern emerges in the shared space, indicating the perpendicular bisector of AB as a locus of points, with ever-increasing clarity (Fig. 2b).

Of course, a dynamic geometry environment can provide this representation on an individual's screen. However, the socially distributed nature of the locus of points in this activity provides an important experience and tool for thinking for the

---

[2]If the class contains fewer than 25 or so students, the activity can be modified to allow students to mark or stamp their point at two or more locations that satisfy the condition.

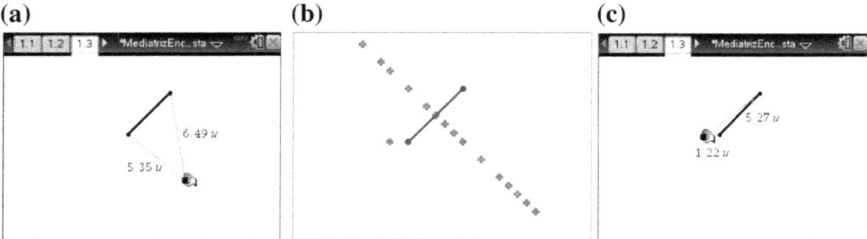

Fig. 2 a, c Students search for points for which the two variable sides of the triangle are of equal length (i.e., which are equidistant from the endpoints of the segment shown in *bold*). **b** The perpendicular bisector emerges as the locus of such points in the shared space

classroom group. As individuals, they have "felt their way around" the Cartesian space, searching for points that meet the equidistant criterion. On finding one, they recognize an isosceles triangle and experience a particular sensation of symmetry. However, based on their own point-based explorations, they can see each of the points in the shared space as a solution to a local problem. This supports a deep and flexible way of thinking about the locus of points and the perpendicular bisector, which has value beyond that which would be gained from the individual experience of a dynamic geometry environment alone.

2.1.8 Conclusion: Mathematical Cyborgs

In speaking of mediated action, we have suggested that human culture is constituted and extended through the creative production of cognitive and symbolic tools. These tools express ways of being in the world, and once internalized, they transform how people perceive and conceive of their worlds. Thus, humans are essentially cyborgs: biological beings who express themselves through tools. In particular, we are already behaving as cyborgs when we engage even in "traditional" mathematical thinking, leveraging the power of Arabic numerals, of the Cartesian system, and so forth.

But we have emphasized the power and interest of dynamic and distributed representations to support new ways of learning how to think and operate with the symbolic entities of mathematics. In the classroom, co-action and the integration of artifact + learner, open the potential to democratize access to these powerful ways of operating with representations. Instrumental genesis, we argue, should be a keystone in the design of new digital curricula that take full advantage of these opportunities. International efforts show ample evidence that this process has already begun. However, school cultures are expressed through institutional forms that have developed over centuries and that are not well adapted to the rapid changes characteristic of new technologies. Engaging in the mathematics of co-action requires a gradual but permanent re-orientation of classroom and school practices, and of the cognitive and epistemological assumptions that underlie them. Our argument here is that as members of a society in which mediated action is deeply entrenched and constitutive, humans are always-already cyborgs. Thus the question is not whether to involve learners in symbiotic relations with technologies, but rather which technologies to choose for which purposes, and how to integrate them, so as to maximize all students' agency.

2.2 The Role of New Technologies: Changing Interactions

The integration of communicational and representational infrastructures can yield forms of representational expressivity (Hegedus and Moreno-Armella 2009), including gestures, new forms of physical interactions, sharing of a product of activity, and verbal forms of communication in which students can engage in. The questions for educational researchers and designers of curricular activities will be how to take advantage of these rich infrastructures (through design with attention given to multimodal affordances) to provide opportunities for learning and meaning making while keeping the student (the learner and user) central to the activity and design. By utilizing the ways in which students (learners) interact with representations of their world, and with one another in the development or design of mathematical activities, digital technologies keep the student central, as authors of their mathematical activity, and the activities of the learners incorporate aspects of their natural function of interaction.

2.2.1 Advances in Activity Spaces

Advances in Activity Spaces have occurred in two broad areas in mathematics education. We investigate both of these with respect to the research and findings conducted as well as offering some concrete examples. First, we look at intentional design in Dynamic Geometry Environments (DGEs) where we posit there has been a trend through the history of DGE implementation of a move towards different forms of activity spaces. This began with construction-heavy based approaches to secondary and post-secondary mathematics to construction-light activities minimizing interface controls and limiting user-drag action to focus the attention of the learner on what is variant or invariant in a well-defined configuration. Such interactions enhance the role of semiotic mediation as one which potentially offers the interactor to "make visible" the hidden mathematical structure or embedded rules. Second, we look at classroom connectivity and how such environments allow the passing and sharing of mathematical artefacts across devices through networks that offer shifts between personal workspaces to public spaces aggregating "pictures of contributions" for whole-class examination and discussing generalizations of mathematical concepts.

Intentional design in DGE

The activity within a DGE has a didactic dimension that transforms the tasks by taking the features and affordances of the dynamic representations into account in activity design (Laborde and Laborde 2014). This purposeful structure of the activity can focus the attention of the learner. The drag tool, or trace feature for example, serve as important tools in design of explorative tasks and can direct learner attention to variant and invariant properties of a mathematical object. A further move in intentional design in DGE's has led to utilizing touch-screen devices enabling individuals to work in a way that is aligned with their out-of-class interactions with touch-screen technologies. Not all use of DGEs on a touch-screen device fully capture the affordances of the DGE. For example, the possibility for mathematical construction is not available in SketchPad Explorer for the iPad, however the possibility of using more than one digit on the screen to interact with the activity sketch, and interact with other students or the teacher in the manipulation of a mathematical object, adds potential to this type of design and the activities that could be developed for such an environment. For example, in work using a DGE to understand the notion of function, Falcade et al. (2007) utilized the dragging and trace tool in the design of activities which have a direct correspondence between the tools of the DGE and the meanings related to the idea of function. The implementation of these designed activities enabled students to explore functional relationships and move towards using the tool to deliberately solve a new problem. Additional work involving DGEs include specific designed activities within the environment for different purposes but to take advantage of specific tools or affordances within the environment and to direct the attention of the learner, (see Ng and Sinclair 2015; Arzarello et al. 2014).

As an example, the authors draw upon work using Sketchpad Explorer for the iPad in which four related activities were designed to allow for a deeper investigation of properties of four triangle centers (circumcenter, centroid, incenter, and orthocenter) and relationships between triangles and these center points. These activities were designed for a small group of students to engage with the tasks and each activity was composed of multiple shorter tasks. The shorter tasks within a broader activity, led to cycles of small group work followed by whole class discussion followed again by small group work. As an example, the third activity explores the incenter through four smaller tasks. In the first task students are exploring the location of the incenter (which is already constructed) for various types of triangles and differentiating it from the previously explored centroid and the circumcenter. In the second task the three angle bisectors are constructed in the sketch and analyzed for various types of triangles through dragging the vertices to create different types of triangles. The trace feature is also utilized to trace the location of the incenter. The third task introduces a grid space to focus attention on the relationship between the distances from the incenter to the sides of the triangle. In the fourth task, students are estimating a circle inscribed inside a triangle, and responding to questions about the relationship between this circle and the triangle and how the circle relates to the incenter. As an example from the classroom in the

Fig. 3 Screen capture where
a vertex (P) of a triangle has
been dragged while the
incenter (S) leaves a trace on
the angle bisector ray
(*orange*)

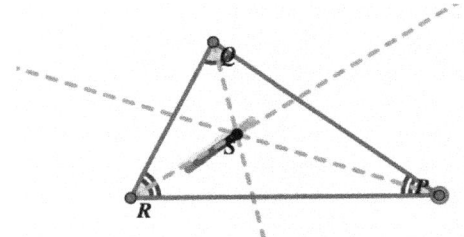

second task the teacher is editing with a group and draws their attention to the differences in the trace marks when one vertex is changed versus when multiple vertices are changed simultaneously.

Teacher: Now, did you notice when you had the trace, like … if I move one of these [the teacher starts moving a single vertex of the triangle horizontally on the iPad while students observe the trace of Point S, the incenter, left behind, see Fig. 3], see it stays on the line [angle bisector ray].
S1: Yeah. … it won't go off.
Teacher: When you move two of them [the teacher starts moving two vertices simultaneously on the iPad], it goes … totally off.
S2: Awry.

The teacher leaves the group after this discovery in which she has interacted directly with the student device. Through her direction and focus on a particular mathematical relationship exposed by the trace feature, the teacher has utilized the technology to interact with students and potentially mediate their future action by dragging a single vertex point in a purposeful way followed by dragging multiple vertex points in a non-purposeful way to explore this relationship between the incenter and the triangle.

Classroom Connectivity

For the second advancement in activity spaces we focus on classroom connectivity that allow the passing and sharing of mathematical artefacts across devices through networks. This work includes projects such as the SimCalc projects, NetLogo projects, TI-Navigator system projects, and work using Sketchpad Explorer for the iPad with connectivity. These projects have investigated ways to support collaboration in the classroom as well as private versus public in the sharing of mathematical work.

In environments utilizing classroom connectivity there is a consideration for activity design related to the coherence between how a student or small group of students are able to interact with the activity individually or within a pair or small group and how the individual or small group is able to interact with the activity when their contribution is public. In the previously introduced work of the authors using dynamic geometry software to investigate triangle centers in a connected classroom environment, this distance seemed to manifest itself in the discourse. In many instances there was a move from speaking and referencing in a dynamic way about the sketch within the small group to speaking and referencing in a static way about the sketch at the whole class level. In small groups students edited in a dynamic way, sometimes with another person. When contributing their triangle configuration to the teacher, the process of their editing became a static image of their end product. In a whole-class discussion students did not incorporate language around their dynamic manipulation into the mathematical discourse of their contributions. This led to a discrepancy between the ways in which the small groups could interact with the specific mathematical activity and their peers at the group level, and the ways the small groups could interact with their own contributions at the whole class level.

Drawing upon the first task investigating the incenter, students are asked to identify similarities or differences between the circumcenter, centriod, and this new unknown center point (the incenter). In one small group of three, the discourse includes directions to one another on how to move a point, "move around that point" and "maybe if we edit all three vertices, [to a third student] you change that one", intentional statements to one another about the type of triangle to create "make it really obtuse", and statements about what they are finding, "You can make it as obtuse as you want. It doesn't work" and "there is no kind of triangle [where the incenter will be located outside the triangle] it cannot happen". These statements are inextricably linked to the dynamic editing of the group members. In the whole class discussion, however, a single sketch is shown from the work of this group. The display of a single sketch does not capture the various types of interactions the students had with one another and within the activity. The sketch is static and the student justification for their finding summarizes their work together but does not bring to light the forms of interaction of the group to determine their findings. This distance between small group and whole class activity in which connectivity is used to support collaboration in the classroom is something to consider for activity design in this type of environment. There are connected classroom designs that seek to close this distance, such as the NetLogo work (Wilensky and Stroup 1999) and the TI-Navigator work (Stroup et al. 2005; White et al. 2012).

The SimCalc project has spent more than 15 years investigating the impact of combining representational affordances of the SimCalc software and connectivity affordances (Hegedus and Roschelle 2012). Classroom connectivity reformats the interaction patterns between students, teachers and technology. This work stresses the importance of the student experience being mathematical. As students participate in mathematical ways, ownership of their constructions can become personal and deeply affective, triggering various forms of interaction after their work is shared and projected into a public display space. As an example, we pull from an activity in an Algebra 2 course in high school in which students are investigating mathematics of change for second-degree functions, their representations, and the role of the parameters "a", "b", and "c" in $y = ax^2 + bx + c$. The mathematical aims of this activity include: investigating varying rate, interpreting the x-intercepts of a linear velocity function as a change in direction in position and associated vertex point of a parabolic position graph, and solving a problem set in a motion context. These aims link connections between position and velocity across various representations. In this activity, the representations available to the student are limited to focus attention on specific relationships between position and velocity. Students work in small groups of four where the parameter "c" corresponds to their group number, given as the starting position of a rocket traveling in space and the acceleration for the rockets is invariant across groups, i.e. "2a". Small group work on a TI-graphing calculator is sent to the teacher via a classroom network and all representations are available for the teacher to display. Before displaying student work, students are asked to make conjectures about the family of functions created in both a position versus time context and a velocity versus time context given they have utilized representations from each. In this way, students are asked to abstract from the specific work of the small group to something more general that would describe all groups in the class. They have ownership over an individual contribution, but this individual contribution is now a piece of the whole in which, together, the class aims to make sense of in terms of the mathematical goals of the activity. This structure of the environment in a connected classroom plays a central participatory role and supports co-action (Moreno-Armella and Hegedus 2009) between the students and the representational affordances of the software.

2.2.2 Multimodality

With the addition of multi-modal devices in various domains, there are new opportunities for designing tools and instructional activities that can leverage gestural resources and additional modes of interaction with mathematics to overall support student learning. In their work investigating haptic force feedback devices for education Güçler et al. (2012) exploited the technological affordances of force-feedback devices to touch and feel attributes of shapes as well as allow students to directly manipulate complex mathematical constructions in simple and successively iterative ways. The authors investigated how learning experiences can be created by the integration of dynamic geometry with new haptic hardware as a multi-modal environment. Multi-modal approaches have also focused on the role of gesture and mathematical expressivity. The work of Güçler et al. (2012) has also explored conceptual benefits of adding direct touch and feedback to dynamic figures in order to explore the meditational effects through discourse.

New technologies taking advantage of multimodality will increase and evolve over the next decade. These types of technology will allow students and teachers to use various sensory modalities (e.g., sight, touch, sound) in their mathematical work and will link or connect the various sensory modalities to help transform the landscape of mathematical inquiry. These types of technologies also have offerings to students with disabilities or of limited modalities. For instance Toennies et al. (2011) describe initial feasibility studies in their paper on use of haptic touchscreen devices to convey graphical and mathematical concepts to students with visual impairments. The authors use auditory and vibratory tactile feedback in the teaching

(a)   (b)

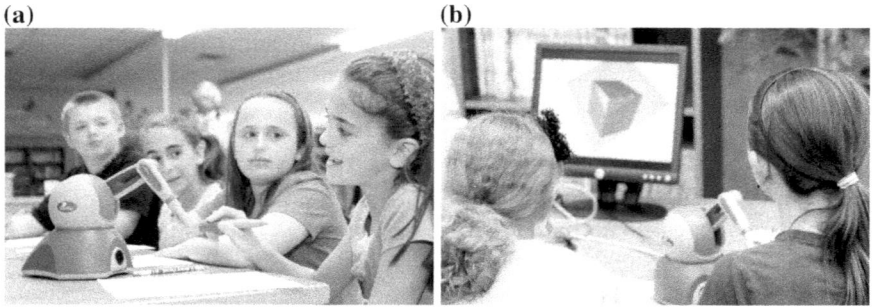

Fig. 4 a A student operates the PHANTOM Omni® haptic device. **b** Students' view of the multi-modal environment

of mathematical concepts that are traditionally taught through a visual modality only. Their initial results indicate that both sensory channels can be valuable in user perception. Recent studies (Güçler et al. 2012) have defined new forms of inter-action that establish access routes for students to explore mathematical structures through multiple modalities. In the example below young learners are utilizing the Geomagic® Touch™ Haptic device (formerly Sensable's PHANTOM Omni® Fig. 4a, b). User interactions with the models within a scene are graphically dis-played through the haptic pointer on the computer screen; and physically meditated by the haptic device, by moving the haptic stylus or pressing the buttons on the stylus. In the application, when a user moves the haptic pointer onto the frictional surface of the cube and presses a haptic button, the position and rotation of the cube is synced to those values of the haptic stylus until the button is released. Learners have the opportunity to physically interact and focus on mathematically important attributes. In our studies (Hegedus and Tall 2015), students offer a variety of metaphors and discursive moves in making sense of complex mathematical surfaces.

2.2.3 From Outside to Inside the Classroom: Augmented Reality

There is work also being done to bridge the gap between technology used outside of an educational setting and the technology used inside an educational setting. The work of Chris Dede and team on EcoMuve and EcoMobile aim to capitalize on mobile devices as a way to collect data in the world for analysis and discussion in the classroom, or some other educational setting. One could argue this work aims to balance the pragmatic and the epistemic value of technologies linking an individual or groups of individuals with the world around them enabling them to mathematize *their* world, and integrate *their* actions as a connected individual with *their* actions as a classroom student.

We draw on the example of EcoMOBILE (Ecosystems Mobile Outdoor Blended Immersive Learning Environment), which provides a learning experience in which students access virtual information and simulated experiences (Augmented Reality-AR) while immersed in real world ecosystems in students' own area (Kamarainen et al. 2015). This science education project was designed to complement the EcoMUVE curriculum, which is based on Multi-User Virtual Environments (MUVEs) experienced on computers in the classroom. Within the EcoMUVE environment, students investigate ecosystems and collect data in immersive simulated ecosystems. This environment is designed to help students learn the system dynamics and complexity within ecosystems and causal relationships from introducing or changing something to, or within, the system. In their work, students collected data using smartphones from a local field trip to nearby pond and brought their data and field notes back to the classroom for further investigation in the virtual pond within the EcoMUVE system.

In their work in next-generation virtual reality interfaces for mathematics and geometry education Kaufmann and Schmalstieg (2003) developed a three-dimensional geometric construction tool called Construct 3D. The system uses Augmented Reality (AR) to provide a natural setting for face-to-face collaboration between teachers and students. All construction steps are carried out via direct manipulation in 3D using a stylus tracked with six degrees of freedom. AR affords users to see their own body and hand as well as the effects of their actions while working, so the construction process physically involves the students and resembles handcraft more than traditional computer operation.

The possible opportunities using AR in combination with dynamic geometry components has the possibility to create further advancements in mathematics education research. These advancements could include student interactions with 3D objects in the world that may have a particular feature of interest to be shared and investigated within the classroom.

2.3 Interrelations Between Mathematics and Technology

This state-of-the-art overview is based on reviewed journals, namely the *Journal for Mathematics Teacher Education, Educational Studies in Mathematics, Technology, Knowledge and Learning, ZDM Mathematics Education*, as well as on proceedings of international conferences such as *CERME* congresses, *ICMI* studies, *ICTMA* and research done in this area, especially in Germany, and also well known anthologies, for example *Springer International Handbooks of Education, Encyclopedia of Mathematics Education* or *Handbuch Mathematikdidaktik*. No systematic research is done on interrelations between mathematics and technology but it is a long and intensively discussed topic in papers as can be seen in Drijvers (2014), Artigue (2002), Stacey and Wiliam (2013), Li and Ma (2010), Bardini et al. (2010) or Weigand (2001, 2006). The core area of mathematics education is teaching how to identify and understand mathematical connections and is described in a lot of curricula all over the world (e.g., NCTM 2000). Laborde (2002, p. 312) describes the challenge for using technology therefore:

> This requires teachers to conceive possible interrelations between the new conceptual aspects introduced by technology and the actual curriculum.

By observing those standards (mathematical) knowledge as well as skills should be conveyed, so that Whitehead's request can be complied (Whitehead 1911 found in Schweiger 2010, p. 9):

> This science, as it is presented to young students, must lose its esoteric face. It has to deal with a few general ideas of far-reaching significance in an obvious, immediate and simple way.

Since the introduction of electronic calculators in mathematics education in the 1970's, the discussion of using those aids has been ongoing. Many studies have been conducted (cf. Barzel 2012) and many questions have been surveyed:

- Which specifications are necessary for designing tasks in mathematics education as well as in mathematics assessments by considering technology?
- How is it possible to work meaningfully in mathematics classrooms by using technology?
- Is it possible to raise the motivation for discussing mathematical problems by using technology in mathematics education?
- Where is it possible to identify mathematics in everyday life and what is the role of technology?
- Is it possible to form another picture of mathematics when using technology in mathematics education?
- How does the use of technology influence mathematical skills and competencies of students?

It is beyond controversy that the use of technology broadens the palette of tools in mathematics education. By using digital tools as a black-box (cf. Buchberger 1989), complex and real problems can be discussed (cf. Rousseau and Saint Aubin 2008). Besides real-life applications, problems of everyday life that do not have an explicit connection to mathematics can be discussed (cf. Siller 2015). Meaningful questions like evacuating a special region or a football stadium, finding the optimal path on a mountain or position-planning can be discussed because the complex mathematical part and the mathematical solution can be outsourced to technology. There are only the personal requirements of identifying and understanding mathematical connections and applying mathematical skills. These are the (new) challenges in mathematics education. Laborde (2002, p. 285) writes:

> When a new element such as technology is introduced, the system is perturbed and has to make choices to ensure a new equilibrium is attained, choices that may be related to the various interrelated elements of the teaching system mentioned [...].

Mathematical objects are changed by the mediation of the digital technology, which gets obvious in dynamic geometry as Laborde (2007) or Gawlick (2002) mentions: dynamic representations of geometrical objects do not exist in the axiomatics of geometry, they are new objects with new behaviours. Digital technologies in mathematics are technologies of a new type; they embody mathematical knowledge.

2.3.1 Digital Tools

Mathematics education is characterized by a high conceptual standard in regard to the development of central terms and through the construction of numerous algorithmic processes. In both areas, great importance can be attached to the use of digital mathematics tools.

Thus, the learning process of the formation of concepts can be supported by visualization at the symbolic, graphical and numerical level. Through the interactivity of the representation levels and the transfer between them, comprehensive multimodal ideas about concepts and their properties can be developed. On the other hand, calculative computations, e.g. calculating the zero points or the determination of primitives, can be outsourced to digital tools. This way, teaching mathematics can be relieved of performing arithmetic operations, and priorities can be set in other areas. However, such 'outsourcing' should be considered thoroughly, because a comprehensive management of calculations has to be given top priority in mathematics education.

Digital tools are not only a pedagogical medium for organizing processes in education, in particular they strengthen the activity of doing mathematics, such as experimenting, visualizing, applying, etc.—cf. Barzel et al. (2005) or Weigand and Weth (2002).

It is a didactic and methodological question when and how digital tools should be used in the teaching process (cf. Weth 1999). For this, there are no standard guidelines; the answer to this question rather depends on the goals that shall be achieved in the teaching process. For example when calculating the square root according to the Heron method, it makes sense to carry out the first steps of this iterative method by hand. The aim is to understand the basic ideas of the process, to reflect on accuracy and limitations and to think about generalizations. The explicit implementation of the method can then be carried out, for instance, by using a spreadsheet.

According to a well-considered use of technology, learning in the classroom is not being degraded to programmed instruction. The tools used are and will remain cognitive tools. They help to represent and work on the individual problem (after input by the person that is working on them). The work on this should be designed so that it supports the mental processes of the learners, who control the learning process, however, they should by no means be restricted. Another important point is 'platform independence'. It should be possible to carry out the tasks on the computer as well as on graphing-capable calculators (with CAS). The technology takes over a large part of the repetitive calculations; graphical and interactive presentation forms are available at an impressive scope. This leaves more time for essential mathematical skills, e.g. interpreting, reflecting, arguing and also modeling or model building for which there is mostly no time in traditional teaching.

In the German educational standards (KMK 2012, p. 13), the importance of digital mathematics tools for the development of mathematical skills is being specified:

"The potential of these tools unfolds in mathematics education

- when exploring mathematical interrelations, in particular through interactive exploration during modeling and problem solving;
- by promoting the understanding of mathematical interrelations, not least through a variety of representation options;
- with the reduction of schematic processes and the processing of large amounts of data;
- by supporting individual preferences and approaches when working on tasks including the reflected use of control options."

2.3.2 Discovering Mathematical Correlations

In view of the discovery of mathematical interrelations, digital mathematics tools are of particular importance for example in simulations, understood as experimenting with models (cf. Greefrath and Weigand 2012). Here, experiments are carried out on a real or mathematical model, e.g. in relation to population trends, traffic situations, or the functionality of technical devices. The use of technology can lead to the simplification of difficult and complex modeling operations, especially when solving, as Galbraith et al. (2003, p.114) has shown (Fig. 5). Sometimes it is even unavoidable to use technological tools, especially when computing-intensive or random processes are being studied, when one wants to structure or process large data sets, when varying processes and results are being displayed, or when one is working experimentally. Especially in the teaching process, deep rethinking of the use of technology is necessary. Traditional content can be discussed with students, however, the use of technological aids also calls for new examples that will be discussed in the classroom using a variety of technologies, and that, at best, lead to different models.

Those models have to be evaluated concerning their quality. Normally this is done through simulations, which can be implemented in, and executed by, technology. By the help of such simulations the process of modelling can be supported as well. Especially if a corresponding reference to reality is being examined, simulations can support the design of varying, more elaborated models (cf. Siller 2015). Here, real situations are chosen as a starting point and a mathematical description of the situation for further examination is generated with the help of models. Geiger (2011, p. 312) shows this analogously to Fig. 6. Monaghan (2004, p. 243f) describes this situation following Kent (1999):

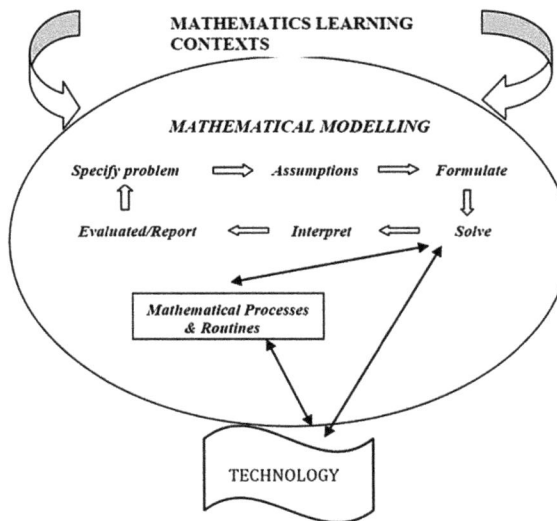

Fig. 5 Using technology when working on problems for mathematical modelling

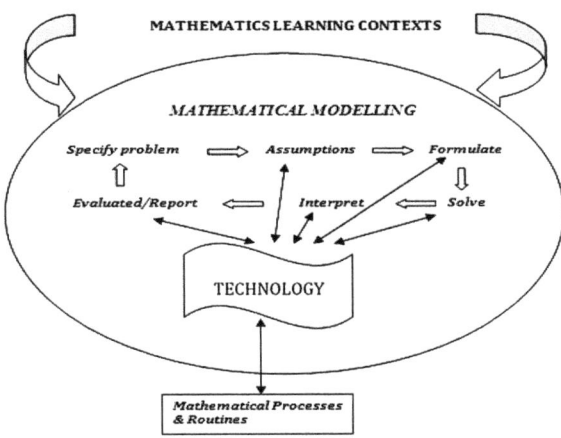

Fig. 6 Mathematical Modelling including the use of technology

This appears to be an important general difference concerning technology lessons and it interrelates with the fact that technology is often not just a tool for doing the mathematics but a medium for expressing the mathematics.

The use of technology allows a 'flexible' handling of problems because routine procedures can be delegated to the 'number cruncher'. Dörfler and Blum (1989, p. 184) mention this at the beginning of the discussion about the use of technological tools in the classroom:

As a mathematical tool, the computer initially allows a relief of the execution of calculatory computations or routine drawings, which can also be a great advantage particularly for an application orientation.

This epistemic dimension of using techniques introduced by digital tools leads students to deepen their conceptual understanding of mathematical objects they involve, as Artigue (2002) or Heid and Blume (2008) has shown.

2.3.3 Possibilities and Constraints in the Interrelation of Technology and Mathematics

Despite all the (possible) advantages the use of technology brings, they should be used in a reflected and considerate way. If technology is used merely as a means to an end, and students do not have to give any feedback on mathematical processes or solutions they have used, the use of technology will not make any sense at all. Nevertheless, the use of digital tools in education offers a lot of different opportunities for routines in mathematics education (cf. Greefrath et al. 2016).

• Use of representation options

With digital mathematics tools, various representations can be produced 'at your fingertips'—it is possible to easily switch between representations (cf. Kaput 2001) and, at the same time, multiple representations can be produced on the screen that are also interactively linked (Weigand and Weth 2002, p. 36 f). These technical possibilities are offset by the challenge of the learning process, which is that students have to cognitively cope with this variety of representations and visualizations in order to use them for a better understanding of mathematical content (Bartolini Bussi and Mariotti 2008).

For example, functions can be represented symbolically, graphically and numerically. When using a computer algebra system, automatic transformations on the symbolic level receive a greater importance; with function plotters, the effects of changes in the functional equation can be graphically traced; and the use of a spreadsheet in particular allows the local visualization of gradual boundary processes at the numerical level. This variety of representations must be cognitively assembled into a mental model by students (see for example, Falcade et al. 2007; Ekol 2015).

• Reduction of schematic processes

Especially through the use of computer algebra systems (CAS), a reduction of schematic processes can be achieved. By this, an overemphasis on calculation-oriented work (e.g., in 'curve sketching') can be countered with CAS. Here, setting up functional equations and the interpretation of the solutions will have an increased importance, whereas the algorithmic calculations are being performed automatically. With this, the target in the classroom is, and has to be, connected to giving central mathematical ways of thinking a more important meaning.

- Checking options

Monitoring and checking the resulting solutions is an important mathematical activity. Digital mathematics tools can support these checking processes, for example with graphical representations of numerical calculations, when solving equations, with term conversions or when working with discrete functional models.

2.3.4 Conclusion

In summary there is an important and remarkable interrelation of mathematics and technology:

- graphical and numerical methods are given more weight;
- substantive concepts on the formation of notions are important, whereby the construction of basic notions and their use play a central role in appropriate problem situations;
- modeling gains importance by a greater variety of available methods for the use of mathematics and for working with mathematical models, for instance in terms of discrete and continuous processes or the function types used;
- a clarification of the technical language in terms of constructive communication with the digital tools is necessary;
- the documentation of results becomes increasingly important as results supplied by the computer have of course to be noted comprehensively for others;
- experimental methods continue to gain importance because the operating principle comes up frequently in the form of typical questions like 'What if …?' or 'Why is it that …?'.

As written by Waits (2000, quotation in NCTM 2000, p. 25):

> Some mathematics becomes more important because technology requires it. Some mathematics becomes less important because technology replaces it. Some mathematics becomes possible because technology allows it.

Students learn to work in a structured way, modularize mathematical tasks, use representation options, verbalize and are able to use the mathematical syntax—in short: students learn to prescind.

Technology can be used for promoting essential competencies as described in Siller (2011). In summary, the learning process changes to an experimental way of awareness when teachers are aware of the interrelations between mathematics and technology.

The use of technology allows students multifaceted findings, which are uncontroversial when using those tools. Hence mathematics becomes more meaningful and more respected. Digital technology relieves students from routines or algorithmic processes. But in the same way it introduces new techniques that the students need to use. These techniques have both an epistemic and pragmatic value according to Artigue (2002). It is important for teaching mathematics with technology that these techniques are coherent with the mathematical content that is taught. Researchers must provide analyses of this underlying epistemology in order to make teachers aware of it.

2.4 Teacher Education with Technology: What, How and Why?

2.4.1 Introduction

This report is based on a review of research papers published during the last fifteen years in four leading journals in mathematics education: *Journal for Mathematics Teacher Education, Educational Studies in Mathematics, Technology, Knowledge and Learning (formerly International Journal of Computers in Mathematics Learning), and ZDM Mathematics Education*, as well as in proceedings of major international conferences in this area: technology groups at CERME 3–9 congresses, ICTMT 10 and 11 conferences and ICMI studies 1 and 17. A selection of forty or so papers considered as relevant to this overview were analyzed. Clearly, we do not claim to have done an exhaustive search, yet we can deem that these papers are representative of current trends in research on teacher education.

Some of the studies address prospective mathematics teacher education, while others focus rather on professional development of practicing mathematics teachers, and we consider both. This paper is organized around the following four questions from the point of view of integrating technology to upper secondary mathematics instruction: (1) What knowledge and skills do the teachers need to efficiently use technology? (2) How these knowledge and skills can be developed in teachers? (3) How do researchers design their studies to follow teachers' development? and (4) What theoretical frameworks inform the research in teacher education? The concluding section brings to the fore issues highlighted in the literature review that seem worth being addressed in the TSG 43.

2.4.2 Knowledge and Skills Teachers Need to Efficiently Use Technology in Upper Secondary Mathematics Classes

When considering teacher education, the question of teacher professional knowledge and skills to be learnt or developed comes up naturally. We address this issue both from the institutional and the research points of view.

Institutional point of view: ICT standards

The ISTE[3] Standards-T (2008) define five skills teachers *"need to teach, work and learn in the digital age"*. They are rather general related to various aspects of a teacher profession:

> (1) "Teachers use their knowledge of subject matter, teaching and learning, and technology to facilitate experiences that advance student learning, creativity, and innovation", (2) "Teachers design, develop, and evaluate authentic learning experiences and assessments incorporating contemporary tools and resources", (3) "Teachers exhibit knowledge, skills, and work processes representative of an innovative professional", (4) Teachers [...] exhibit legal and ethical behavior in their professional practices, and (5) "Teachers continuously improve their professional practice [...], exhibit leadership in their school and professional community by promoting and demonstrating the effective use of digital tools and resources".

NCTM (2011) claims that

> Programs in teacher education and professional development must continually update practitioners' knowledge of technology and its application to support learning. This work with practitioners should include the development of mathematics lessons that take advantage of technology-rich environments and the integration of digital tools in daily instruction, instilling an appreciation for the power of technology and its potential impact on students' understanding and use of mathematics.

This NCTM position emphasizes three conditions for an efficient integration of technology, which should guide the development of teacher education programs: teachers' awareness of the technology added value in terms of students' understanding of mathematics, teachers' continuous upgrading of their knowledge of technology and its use in teaching, and designing teaching resources taking advantage of affordances of digital tools.

UNESCO ICT Competency Framework for Teachers (2011) sets out *"the competencies required to teach effectively with ICT"* (p. 3) and stresses that

> it is not enough for teachers to have ICT competencies and be able to teach them to their students. Teachers need to be able to help the students become collaborative, problem solving, creative learners through using ICT so they will be effective citizens and members of the workforce (ibid.)

The Framework is organized around three stages of ICT integration: (1) Technology Literacy *"enabling students to use ICT in order to learn more efficiently"*, (2) Knowledge Deepening *"enabling students to acquire in-depth knowledge of their school subjects and apply it to complex, real-world problems"*, and (3) Knowledge Creation *"enabling students, citizens and the workforce they become, to create the new knowledge required for more [...] prosperous societies"* (p. 3). Examples of methods for professional learning of skills related to each aspect of teachers' work (understanding ICT in education, curriculum and assessment,

---

[3]International Society for Technology in Education, http://iste.org.

pedagogy, ICT, organization and administration, and teacher professional learning) at the three stages are provided.

The above mentioned standards (except from NCTM) are usually not subject matter specific. The NCTM standards have the merit of stressing the importance of teachers' awareness of the technology added value for students' learning mathematics as a first step toward an efficient ICT use.

Research point of view: professional knowledge and skills addressed in scientific papers

In this section we attempt to synthesize what professional competencies are considered by the researchers as important for using ICT by mathematics teachers. Surprisingly, references to standards, either national or international, are very rare. Only Bowers and Stephens (2011) mention the NCTM (2000) "Technology Principle": each teacher should use technology in "*appropriate and responsible ways*" (p. 286), which the authors interpret as "*using technology to explore mathematical relations.*" (ibid.).

The *Technology, Pedagogy and Content Knowledge* (TPACK) framework (Mishra and Koehler 2006) is the most frequently used frame that offers "*a helpful way to conceptualize what knowledge prospective teachers need in order to integrate technology into teaching practices*" (Bowers and Stephens ibid). However, this framework allows for a variety of interpretations. While some authors attempt to define specific TPACK knowledge pieces, others consider the TPACK rather as an orientation enabling the teacher educators "*to develop a greater sense of how to plan and focus instruction for prospective math teachers*" (ibid. p. 301). The former approach is adopted by Robová (2013) who defines what she calls "*Specific Skills for work in GeoGebra*", and she proposes a set of such skills instantiated to the case of functions: e.g., "*making functions visible (on the screen)*" or "*using dynamic features of GeoGebra*". The latter approach is advocated by Bowers and Stephens (2011), who draw on literature review to claim that

> teachers need not acquire one particular expertise or pick one particular role; instead, teachers (and prospective teachers) need to become aware of how to design rich tasks that integrate technology into the classroom discourse so that technology-based conjectures and arguments become normative (p. 290).

Although most research is inscribed within a specific context linking a mathematics domain and a type of technology at stake, three different approaches to defining teachers' knowledge and skills related to the technology use can be identified:

- setting out knowledge/skills needed to teach a particular mathematical concept or area with technology, such as functions (Borba 2012) or algebra (Clay et al. 2012);
- setting out knowledge/skills required to use a particular piece of software, such as CAS (Ball 2004; Zehavi and Mann 2011) or dynamic geometry (Robová 2013; Robová and Vondrová 2015),

- considering more general knowledge/skills, such as the ability of supporting students' problem solving in a technological environment (Lee 2005), of analyzing digital resources in order to evaluate their pedagogical affordances and relevance (Trgalová and Jahn 2013), of encouraging students to use a tool of their choice to observe mathematical relations at stake (Bowers and Stephens 2011) or of using ICT to develop reasoning capacities in students (Zuccheri 2003).

2.4.3 How These Knowledge and Skills Can Be Developed in Teachers?

A growing interest in delivering teacher education courses via online platforms is observed: a small number of professional development courses use both synchronic and/or a-synchronic internet platforms blended with face-to-face meetings (e.g., Clark-Wilson et al. 2015; Borba 2012; Bowers and Stephens 2011). Most of the courses use either face-to-face platform (e.g., Lee 2005) or online platform (e.g., Clay et al. 2012).

Several researchers consider creating communities of practice, composed of teachers with different expertise, as a relevant platform for teachers' development. Thus, for example, Zehavi and Mann (2011) report on face-to-face collaboration between course instructors and participating teachers: at first the activity was guided by the instructors, however the use of unusual mathematical results in CAS environment caused the novice participants to raise a mathematical challenge which was resolved together, in a way that promoted the mathematical knowledge of all the community. Borba and Llinares (2012) provide an overview of online teacher education centered on creating communities of practice. Specifically, in a-synchronic communications, participants with different expertise are encouraged to express their ideas and relate to others' ideas. By written reflections and elaborations of these ideas, all members deepen their pedagogical and mathematical insights.

Many professional development opportunities are organized around iterative sequences of activities of different nature. Lee (2005) uses a sequence of planning a mathematical activity with technology for students, experiencing as facilitators of that activity with a pair of students reflection on the design versus enactment of the activity. The sequence was repeated twice for each prospective teacher, to allow for changes in all three phases. While Lee studies a face-to-face course, Clay et al. (2012) report on an online course: a more refined sequence of activities, starting with setting a mathematical goal and designing a related set of tasks by the instructor, and inviting participants to perform the following activities:

(1) reviewing an expert model, (2) creating initial responses to the task (in the form of a multimedia screen capture with voice), (3) listening to/viewing others' responses, (4) reviewing and commenting on others' responses, (5) discussing, and (6) revising initial responses. (p. 765).

Only few studies include an evaluation of the reported professional development. Robová and Vondrová (2015—to appear) use teachers' final project quality as evidence for the success of instruction, reporting that "*Still, the quality of the preservice teachers' projects did not meet our expectation*". Zuccheri (2003) also notes her dissatisfaction: "*They seem to give attention only to partial aspects of the didactical use of the software, or to technical aspects, or to enjoying the use of the tool itself*".

A similar dissatisfaction led Emprin (2007) to analyze training courses aimed at the use of ICT by means of interviews with teacher educators and observations in several professional development courses. Emprin (2007) claims that the main reason is a gap between teachers' needs and potentialities presented by teacher trainers during professional development courses. Specifically, he notes a lack of reflectively analyzing the complexity of practice.

One exceptional study in terms of evaluating the program was done by Jiang et al. (2013). The authors randomly assigned 64 high school teachers to two groups, both studying geometry: one learned with technology and the other without. A pre-post design allowed the authors to report that teachers who learned with dynamic geometry (DG) scored higher in conjecturing and proving compared to teachers who learned in a traditional environment. Moreover, a geometry achievement pre- and post-tests applied on students of all participating teachers show that students of the teachers who learned in DG environment significantly outperformed those of the other teachers.

2.4.4 How Do Researchers Design Their Studies to Follow Teachers' Development?

Case studies are the dominant methodology used. The studies were cases of: (1) one specific course, and (2) specific issue from a particular course, like a specific activity, or the work done by specific participants. Usually, the authors are among the professional development leaders. For example, Sacristán et al. (2011) report on professional development program which was an integral part of six teachers' dissertation for MA program, in which the participants reflect on their experience of integrating ICT to their own teaching. Lee (2005) describes her qualitative methodology which includes analyzing videos and comparing cases to look for patterns.

Among studies with a different methodology, Tripconey et al. (2013) provide one-day training course to practicing teachers with two types of training: one devoted to exploring ICT packages while the other focusing on developing specific subject knowledge, incorporating ideas for using ICT. The researchers were interested in changes in teachers' ICT uses in their class after the one-day training course. A written questionnaire was sent via the internet asking the teachers to report if they used ICT for math teaching. In both groups there was a slight increase in the number of teachers using ICT to demonstrate in class. The ICT specific group seemed to have a marginally greater increase. However, the researchers concluded that for the majority of teachers there was no change in all surveyed categories in the amount of time they used ICT. It appears that the impact of a one-day course, albeit ICT focused or incorporated, is limited.

Clark-Wilson et al. (2015) try to find a method to follow a large group of teachers from 113 schools in an attempt to evaluate the teachers' fidelity to a specific learning unit. They used teachers' self-report questionnaire to evaluate teachers' fidelity to their program, accompanied by two case studies. The authors discuss the limitations of such approach, both in terms of a low rate of responses, and the subjectivity of the reports. Nevertheless, they could get insight in the way teachers and schools appropriated the use of ICT with the specific curriculum to be implemented.

Yet another approach was taken by Trgalová and Jahn (2013). The authors were concerned with teachers' ability to identify from the growing collection of online resources the ones most relevant to their educational needs. They designed a quality questionnaire for the i2geo repository aiming at framing the analysis of available resources by the platform users. Their study thus focused on teachers' changing ability to evaluate online resources and their changes in practices stemming from their awareness of the quality criteria.

2.4.5 Why the Researchers Acted the Way They Did

This section focuses on theoretical grounding of research papers on teacher education. The *TPACK framework* has already been mentioned.

Besides TPACK, there is a big variety of theoretical frames, some of which are specific to technology while others are more general, such as the anthropological theory of didactics (Chevallard 1992) or the theory of semiotic registers of representation (Duval 2006). Most of research draws on a combination of two or more theoretical frames showing that the technology element should not be taken separately but rather as an element of a whole system composed of actors (students and teacher), knowledge at stake and a set of other resources coming into play in teaching and learning mathematics.

Among the technology specific frameworks, the *instrumental approach* (Rabardel 2002) is certainly the most widely used. Elaborated in the field of cognitive ergonomics, it brings to the fore the acknowledgment of the importance of a person's activity with a tool rather than considering uses guided by the tool. This framework further developed within mathematics education (Artigue 2002) led to the introduction of new concepts, e.g., *instrumental orchestration* (Trouche 2004; Drijvers et al. 2010) or *double instrumental genesis* (Haspekian 2011) focusing on teacher's role in managing students' interactions with ICT. The *documentational approach* (Gueudet and Trouche 2009) addressing teachers' work with resources, either digital or not, draws as well on the instrumental approach.

The theoretical concept of *humans-with-media* introduced by Borba and Villareal (2005) sheds light on how technological tools, but also non-technological media, influence and reorganize the way humans know and produce knowledge. This framework is mainly used to address issues related to online pre-service and in-service teacher education (Borba 2012; Clay et al. 2012).

Another concept widely used, mainly in relation with teacher professional development, is the notion of *community*: *community of practice* or *community of inquiry* (Jaworski 2005). Such communities are either created purposefully by the researchers to accompany teachers' efforts with integrating ICT in their everyday practice (e.g., Fuglestad 2007), or they develop spontaneously around Web2.0 tools enabling sharing resources and practices (Trgalová and Jahn 2013). Drawing on the concept of community, researchers mostly address the issue of teachers' learning and development within communities.

2.4.6 Concluding Remarks

The literature review presented above highlights four striking issues. First, ICT competency standards for teachers seem to have limited impact on the orientations of teacher education programs. Certainly these standards are too general, neither subject matter (except from NCTM), nor school level specific. Elaboration of ICT standards for mathematics teacher education might become one of the goals of the international community. The second issue is the acknowledgment, in a number of research papers, of a disappointment with the outcomes of teacher education programs. The gap between teachers' needs and the teacher education contents is deemed as the main reason. This brings to the fore a necessity for teacher educator training, which is an under-represented issue in the field of mathematics education research, as well as a necessity for teacher educators to understand better teachers' needs, which brings back the issue of ICT competency standards. Third, regarding the theoretical frameworks referred to in research papers, a large variety of frames can be noticed, which can be seen as a wealth of the research field, but there is a risk of "*the framework compartmentalization that could hinder the capitalization of knowledge and its practical exploitation*" (Artigue et al. 2011, p. 2381). A development of "*an integrated theoretical framework*" based on networking theories appears as a means "*to support the capitalization of research on digital technologies in mathematics education*" (ibid. p. 2387). Finally, some competencies seem to be under-estimated in teacher education: teachers' ability to decide when it is worth using technology and when it is not, to analyze a piece of software so that the teachers are able to face unwelcome phenomena linked to the computational transposition such as consequences of working with approximate values. We propose these four issues to the discussion in the topic study group 43.

3 Summary and Looking Ahead

- Various research theoretical frameworks are used to analyze the learning and teaching processes.
  Some of them deal with the new ways digital technology mediates mathematical objects and relationships and consider interaction of students and teachers with technology (coaction, humans-with-media). The instrumental approach is used in analyzing both the processes through which students construct solving strategies by making use of technology and the teaching processes. A double instrumental genesis is required from teachers for doing mathematics using technology and for organizing learning conditions through the use of technology for their students, in particular by designing appropriate tasks taking advantage of technology.

- New ways of learning how to think, operate and interact with dynamic and distributed technologies are presented.
  Research studies show that these technologies offer a potential to the learners to interact with mathematical structures, in particular improve the cycle of exploration, conjecture, explanation and justification. It also can offer the opportunity for students to build on the work of another through the ability to share products and problem solving strategies. These dynamic and distributed technologies have a potential to democratize access to powerful mathematical ideas and ways of operating with mathematical symbols and structures.
  A final and significant point is the impact of "new" learning technologies as operationalized through *how we interact* in a learning environment on the mindset of teachers. As Hegedus and Tall (2015) have noted, a long-term critical issue will be the professional development of teachers in order to understand how to use these new tools, take advantage of the affordances and possibilities, and understand the pedagogical implications. Teachers might be faced with re-thinking how technologies can enhance the learning environment or even transform the very nature of the classroom.

- Digital technologies may shift emphasis on some mathematical activities while making others less important

  Modeling, interpreting graphical representations, experimental activities, checking processes gain importance that may lead to critical thinking and creative acting.

- Importance of the teacher in the use of technology
  The role of the teacher is still critical as earlier in absence of the technologies described in our account. However the use of technology may require different skills and competencies as for example: find new ways of introducing concepts with technology, designing new kind of tasks, understanding the new students exploring and solving processes allowed by technology, and using ICT to develop reasoning capacities in their students.

Some thinking points. Practically, for teachers in the classroom: is there, or could there be, a taxonomy for orchestrating student digital work? How can the teacher make best use of student created contributions? What new opportunities of interaction are there between the teacher and the students and what is the role of the teacher within these new forms of interactions? How can the teacher mediate rich interactions between students and content through (or in conjunction with) the technology in order to fully utilize the representational and communicational infrastructure of the classroom?

- Gap between the teachers' needs and the contents of teacher education programs
  Teacher education programs should include more the required skills and competencies that, according to research, teachers need for integrating digital technology into the usual teaching practice.

References

Artigue, M. (2002). Learning mathematics in a CAS environment: The genesis of a re-flection about instrumentation and the dialectics between technical and conceptual work. *International Journal of Computers for Mathematical Learning, 7*, 245–274.

Artigue, M., Bosch, M., & Gascon, J. (2011). Research praxeologies and networking theories. In M. Pylak, et al. (Eds.), *Proceedings of the 7th Congress of the European society for research in mathematics education* (pp. 2381–2390). Poland: University of Rzeszów.

Arzarello, F., Bairral, M. A., & Danè, C. (2014). Moving from dragging to touchscreen: geometrical learning with geometric dynamic software. *Teaching Mathematics and Its Applications, 33*(1), 39–51.

Baldwin, M. (1896). A new factor of evolution. *The American Naturalist 30*, 441–451, 536–553)

Ball, L. (2004). Researchers and teachers working together to deal with the issues, opportunities and challenges of implementing CAS into the senior secondary mathematics classroom. *ZDM—The International Journal on Mathematics Education 36*(1), 27–31.

Bardini, C., Drijvers, P., & Weigand, H. -G. (2010) (Eds.). Handheld technology in the mathematics classroom—theory and practice. *ZDM—The International Journal on Mathematics Education 42*(7).

Bartolini Bussi, M. G., & Mariotti, M. A. (2008). Semiotic mediation in the mathematics classroom: Artifacts and signs after a Vygotskian perspective. In L. English, M. Bartolini Bussi, G. Jones, R. Lesh, & D. Tirosh (Eds.). *Handbook of international research in mathematics education*. Mahwah: Lawrence Erlbaum.

Barzel, B. (2012). *Computeralgebra im Mathematikunterricht. Ein Mehrwert – aber wann?*. Münster: Waxmann Verlag.

Barzel, B., Hußmann, T., & Leuders, T. (2005). *Computer, internet & co. im Mathematik-Unterricht*. Berlin: Scriptor-Cornelsen.

Borba, M. C. (2012), Humans-with-media and continuing education for mathematics teachers in online environments. *ZDM—The International Journal on Mathematics Education 44*, 801–814.

Borba, M. C., & Llinares, S. (2012). Online mathematics teacher education: Overview of an emergent field of research. *ZDM Mathematics Education, 44*, 697–704.

Borba, M. C., & Villarreal, M. (2005). *Humans-with-media and reorganization of mathematical thinking: ICT, modeling, experimentation and visualization*. USA: Springer.

Bowers, J. S., & Stephens, B. (2011). Using technology to explore mathematical relationships: A framework for orienting mathematics courses for prospective teachers. *Journal of Mathematics Teacher Education, 14*, 285–304.

Buchberger, B. (1989). Should students learn integration rules? Technical Report. Linz: RISC (Research Institute for Symbolic Computation).

Chevallard, Y. (1992). Concepts fondamentaux de la didactique: perspectives apportées par une approche anthropologique. *Recherches en Didactique des Mathématiques, 12*(1), 73–112.

Clark-Wilson, A., et al. (2015). Scaling a technology-based innovation: windows on the evolution of mathematics teachers' practices. *ZDM—The International Journal on Mathematics Education 47*, 79–92.

Clay, E., Silverman, J., Fischer, D. J. (2012). Unpacking online asynchronous collaboration in mathematics teacher education. *ZDM—The International Journal on Mathematics Education 44*, 761–773.

Donald, M. (2001). *A mind so rare: The evolution of human consciousness*. New York: Norton.

Dörfler, W. & Blum, W. (1989). Bericht über die Arbeitsgruppe "Auswirkungen auf die Schule". In Maaß, J.; Schlöglmann, W. (Hrsg.), Mathematik als Technologie? - Wechselwirkungen zwischen Mathematik, Neuen Technologien, Aus- und Weiter- bildung (pp. 174–189). Weinheim: Deutscher Studienverlag.

Drijvers, P. (2014). Digital technology in mathematics education: A reflective look into the mirror. In J. Roth & J. Ames (Eds.), *Beiträge zum Mathematikunterricht 2014* (pp. 21–28). Münster: WTM-Verlag.

Drijvers, P., Doorman, M., Boon, P., et al. (2010). The teacher and the tool: instrumental orchestrations in the technology-rich mathematics classroom. *Educational Studies in Mathematics, 75*, 13–234.

Duval, R. (2006). A cognitive analysis of problems of comprehension in a learning of mathematics. *Educational Studies in Mathematics, 61*, 103–131.

Duval, R. (1999). Representation, Vision and Visualization: Cognitive Functions in Mathematical Thinking. Basic Issues for Learning. In F. Hitt, & M. Santos (Eds), *Proceedings of the annual meeting of the north American chapter of the international group for the psychology of mathematics education* (pp. 3–26). Cuernavaca: Mexico.

Ekol, G. (2015). Exploring foundation concepts in introductory statistics using dynamic data points. *International Journal of Education in Mathematics, Science and Technology, 3*(3), 230–241.

Emprin, F. (2007). Analysis of teacher education in mathematics and ICT. In D. Pitta-Pantazi & G. Philippou (Eds.) *Proceedings of the 5th Congress of the European society for research in mathematics education* (pp. 1399–1408), Larnaca: University of Cyprus.

Falcade, R., Laborde, C., & Mariotti, M. A. (2007). Approaching functions: Cabri tools as instruments of semiotic mediation. *Educational Studies in Mathematics, 66*(3), 317–333.

Fuglestad, A. B. (2007). Developing tasks and teaching with ICT in mathematics in an inquiry community. In D. Pitta-Pantazi & G. Philippou (Eds.) *Proceedings of the 5th Congress of the European society for research in mathematics education* (pp. 1409–1418), Larnaca: University of Cyprus.

Galbraith, G. et al. (2003). Technology-enriched classrooms. Some implications for teaching applications and modeling. In Y. Qi-Xiao, W. Blum, S. K. Houston, J. Qi-Yuan (Eds.), *Mathematical modelling in education and culture: ICTMA 10* (p. 111–125). Chichester: Horwood.

Gawlick, T. (2002). On dynamic geometry software in the regular classroom. *Zentralblatt fuer Didaktik der Mathematik, 34*(3), 85–92.

Geiger, V. (2011). Factors affecting teachers' adoption of innovative practices with technology and mathematical modelling. In G. Kaiser, W. Blum, R. Borromeo-Ferri, & G. Stillmann (Eds.). Trends in Teaching and Learning of Mathematical Modelling: ICTMA 14 (pp. 305–315). Heidelberg: Springer.

Gibson, J. J. (2014). *The ecological approach to visual perception.* New York: Psychology Press.

Gleick, J. (1993). *Genius: Richard Feynman and modern physics.* New York: Pantheon.

Greefrath, G., Oldenburg, R., Siller, H-St, Weigand, H.-G., & Ulm, V. (2016). *Didaktik der Analysis.* Wiesbaden: Springer.

Greefrath, G., Weigand, H.-G. (2012). Simulieren: Mit Modellen experimentieren. mathematik lehren, 174, 2–6.

Güçler, B., Hegedus, S., Robidoux, R., & Jackiw, N. (2012). Investigating the mathematical discourse of young learners involved in multi-modal mathematical investigations: The case of haptic technologies. In D. Martinovic, V. Freiman, & Z. Karadag (Eds.), *Visual mathematics and cyberlearning* (pp. 97–118). New York, NY: Springer.

Gueudet, G., & Trouche, L. (2009). Towards new documentation systems for teachers? *Educational Studies in Mathematics, 71*(3), 199–218.

Haspekian, M. (2011). The co-construction of a mathematical and a didactical instrument. In M. Pytlak, T. Rowland, & E. Swoboda (Eds.), *Proceedings of the 7th Congress of the European society for research in mathematics education* (pp. 2298–2307). Rzeszów: University of Rzeszów.

Hegedus, S., & Tall, D. O. (2015). Foundations for the future: The potential of multimodal technologies for learning mathematics. In L. English & D. Kirshner (Eds.), *The third edition of the handbook of international research in mathematics education* (pp. 543–562). New York, NY: Routledge.

Hegedus, S. J., & Moreno-Armella, L. (2009). Intersecting representation and communication infrastructures. *ZDM-The International Journal on Mathematics Education, 41*(4), 399–412.

Hegedus, S. J., & Roschelle, J. (Eds.). (2012). *The simcalc vision and contributions: Democratizing access to important mathematics.* Netherlands: Springer.

Heid, M. K., & Blume, G. W. (2008). Technology and the teaching and learning of mathematics: Cross-content implications. In M. K. Heid & G. W. Blume (Eds.), *Research on technology and the teaching and learning of mathematics: Syntheses, cases, and perspectives* (Vol. 1, pp. 419–431)., Research syntheses Charlotte, NC: Information Age Publishing.

ISTE Standards-T (2008). *ISTE Standards Teachers.* Online http://www.iste.org/standards/iste-standards/standards-for-teachers [Retrieved September 17, 2015]

Jaworski, B. (2005). Learning communities in mathematics: Creating an inquiry community between teachers and didacticians. *Research in Mathematics Education, 7*(1), 101–119.

Jiang, Z., White, A., Sorto, A., & Rosenwasser A. (2013). Investigating the impact of a technology-centered teacher professional department program. In E. Faggiano & A. Montone (Eds.) *Proceedings of the 11th international Conference on technology in mathematics teaching* (pp. 156–161), Bari: University of Bari.

Kamarainen, A. M., Metcalf, S., Grotzer, T.A., & Dede, C. (2015). Exploring ecosystems from the inside: how immersive multi-user virtual environments can support development of epistemologically grounded modeling practices in ecosystem science instruction. *Journal of Science Education and Technology, 24*(2), 148–167.

Kaufmann, H., and Schmalstieg, D. (2003). Mathematics and geometry education with collaborative augmented reality. *Computers & Graphics, 27*(3), 339–345.

Kaput, J. (2001). *Changing representational infrastructures changes most everything: The case of SimCalc algebra, and calculus. Paper presented at the NAS symposium on improving learning with informational technology*. Washington, DC. Available at http://www.kaputcenter.umassd. edu/downloads/simcalc/cc1/library/changinginfrastruct.pdf, Last Access: February 2016.

Kent, P. (1999). *Some notes on expressiveness*. Available at http://www.lkl.ac.uk/research/came/ events/weizmann/Expressiveness-notes.pdf, Last Access: February 2016.

KMK (2012). *Bildungsstandards im Fach Mathematik für die Allgemeine Hochschulreife* (Beschluss der Kultusministerkonferenz vom 18.10.2012). Köln, Wolters Kluwer.

Laborde, C. (2002). Integration of technology in the design of geometry tasks with cabri-geometry. *International Journal of Computers for Mathematical Learning, 6*(3), 283–317.

Laborde, C. (2007). The role and uses of technologies in mathematics classrooms: Between challenge and modus vivendi. *Canadian Journal of Science, Mathematics and Technology Education, 7*(1), 68–92.

Laborde, C., & Laborde, J. M. (2014). Dynamic and tangible representations in mathematics education. *Transformation: A fundamental idea of mathematics education* (pp. 187–202). New York, NY: Springer.

Lee, H. S. (2005). Facilitating students' problem solving in a technological context: Prospective teachers' learning trajectory. *Journal for Mathematics Teacher Education, 8*, 223–254.

Li, Q., & Ma, X. (2010). A meta-analysis of the effects of computer technology on school students' mathematics learning. *Educational Psychology Review, 22*, 215–243.

Mishra, P., & Koehler, M. J. (2006). Technological pedagogical content knowledge: A new framework for teacher knowledge. *Teachers College Record, 108*(6), 1017–1054.

Monaghan, J. (2004). Teachers' activities in technology-based mathematics lesson. *International Journal of Computers for Mathematical Learning, 9*(3), 327–357.

Moreno-Armella, L., & Hegedus, S. J. (2009). Co-action with digital technologies. *ZDM-The International Journal on Mathematics Education, 41*(4), 505–519.

NCTM—National Council of Teachers of Mathematics. (2000). *Principles and standards for school mathematics*. Reston, VA: National Council of Teachers of Mathematics.

NCTM. (2011). *Technology in teaching and learning mathematics. A position of the national council of teachers of mathematics*. Retrieved September 17, 2015 from http://www.nctm.org/ Standards-and-Positions/Position-Statements/Technology-in-Teaching-and-Learning-Mathematics/

Ng, O.-L., & Sinclair, N. (2015). "Area without numbers": Using touchscreen dynamic geometry to reason about shape. *Canadian Journal of Science, Mathematics and Technology Education, 15*(1), 84–101.

Rabardel, P. (1995). *Les hommes et les technologies; approche cognitive des instruments contemporains*. Paris: Armand Colin.

Rabardel, P. (2002). *People and technology—a cognitive approach to contemporary instruments*. Université Paris 8. Retrieved October 15, 2013 from https://hal-univ-paris8.archives-ouvertes. fr/file/index/docid/1020705/filename/people_and_technology.pdf

Robová, J. (2013). Specific skills necessary to work with some ICT tools in mathematics effectively. *Acta Didactica Mathematicae, 35*, 71–104.

Robová, J., & Vondrová, N. (2015—to appear). Developing future mathematics teachers' ability to identify specific skills needed for work in GeoGebra. In K. Krainer & N. Vondrová (Eds.) *Proceedings of the 9th Congress of the European society for research in mathematics education*, Prague: Charles University.

Rousseau, C., & Saint Aubin, Y. (2008). Mathématiques et Technologie. New York: Springer.

Sacristán, A. I., Sandoval, I., & Gil, N. (2011). Teachers engage in peer tutoring and course design inspired by a professional training model for incorporating technologies for mathematics teaching in Mexican schools. In M. Joubert, A. Clark-Wilson & M. McCabe (Eds.) *Proceedings of the 10th International Conference on Technology in Mathematics Teaching* (pp. 248–253), Portsmouth: University of Portsmouth.

Schweiger, F. (2010). *Fundamentale Ideen*. Aachen: Shaker.

Siller, H-St. (2011). Standardisierte Prüfungen – Chance oder Hindernis für einen (sinnvollen) Computereinsatz? *Praxis der Mathematik in der Schule, PM, 39*, 32–35.

Siller, H.-St. (Ed.). (2015). Realitätsbezug im Mathematikunterricht - Themenheft. *Der Mathematikunterricht 5/2015*, Seelze: Friedrich.

Stacey, K., & Wiliam, D. (2013). Technology and assessment in mathematics. In M. A. Clements, A. Bishop, C. Keitel, J. Kilpatrick, & F. Leung (Eds.), *Third international handbook of mathematics education* (pp. 721–751). New York: Springer.

Stroup, W. M., Ares, N. M., & Hurford, A. C. (2005). A dialectic analysis of generativity: Issues of network-supported design in mathematics and science. *Mathematical Thinking and Learning, 7*(3), 181–206.

Toennies, J. L., Burgner, J., Withrow, T. J., & Webster, R. J. (2011, June). Toward haptic/aural touchscreen display of graphical mathematics for the education of blind students. In *World Haptics Conference (WHC)* (pp. 373–378). IEEE.

Trgalová, J. & Jahn, A. P. (2013). Quality issue in the design and use of resources by mathematics teachers. *ZDM—The International Journal on Mathematics Education 45*, 973–986.

Tripconey, S., de Pomerai, S., & Lee, S. (2013). The impact of training courses on mathematics teachers' use of ICT in their classroom practice. In E. Faggiano & A. Montone (Eds.), *Proceedings of the 11th international conference on technology in mathematics teaching* (pp. 274–279), Bari: University of Bari.

Trouche, L. (2004). Managing the complexity of human/machine interactions in computerized learning environments: guiding students' command process through instrumental orchestrations. *International Journal of Computers for Mathematical Learning, 9*, 281–307.

UNESCO ICT Competency Framework for Teachers. (2011). Paris: United Nations Educational, Scientific and Cultural Organization.

Vygotsky, L. (1978). *Mind in society: The development of higher psychological processes*. Cambridge, MA: Harvard University Press.

Weigand, H.-G. (2001). Zur Bedeutung didaktischer Prinzipien im Entschleunigungsprozess beim Lernen mit neuen Technologien. In H.-J. Elschenbroich, T. Gawlick, & H.-W. Henn (Eds.), *Zeichnung – Figur – Zugfigur* (pp. 195–205). Franzbecker: Mathematische und didaktische Aspekte Dynamischer Geometrie-Software, Hildesheim.

Weigand, H.-G. (2006). Der Einsatz eines Taschencomputers in der 10. Klassenstufe - Evaluation eines einjährigen Schulversuchs. *Journal für Mathematik-Didaktik 27*(2), 89–112.

Weigand, H.-G., & Weth, T. (2002). *Computer im Mathematikunterricht: Neue Wege zu alten Zielen*. Heidelberg: Spektrum.

Wertsch, J. V. (1991). *Voices of the mind: A sociological approach to mediated action*. Cambridge, MA: Harvard University Press.

Weth, T. (1999). Der Computer macht's möglich: Geometrische Phänomene entschlüsseln. *Unterrichten und Erziehen, 4*(99), 191–192.

White, T., Wallace, M., & Lai, K. (2012). Graphing in groups: Learning about lines in a collaborative classroom network environment. *Mathematical Thinking and Learning, 14*(2), 149–172.

Whitehead, A. N. (1911). *An introduction to mathematics*. London: Oxford University Press.

Wilensky, U., & Stroup, W. (1999). Participatory simulations: Network-based design for systems learning in classrooms. *Proceedings of the conference on computer-supported collaborative learning*, CSCL'99, Stanford University.

Zehavi, N., & Mann, G. (2011). Development process of a praxeology for supporting the teaching of proofs in a cas environment based on teachers' experience in a professional development course. *Technology, Knowledge, Learning, 16*, 153–181.

Zuccheri, (2003). Problems arising in teachers' education in the use of didactical tools. In M. A. Mariotti (Ed.), *Proceedings of the 3rd conference of the European society for research in mathematics education*. Bellaria: University of Pisa.